CW00739952

Partners
for
Life

Discover the secret
of a Successful Marriage

DEREK PRINCE

PARTNERS FOR LIFE

© 2005 Derek Prince Ministries-International

This edition published by Derek Prince Ministries—UK 2006
This book is an edited transcript of from Keys to Successful Living
radio programme No. 001 "The Key to a Successful Marriage" by
Derek Prince.

ISBN: 978-1-901144-31-4
Product code: T01

Editorial, design and production services by Summit Publishing Ltd.

Printed in the United Kingdom by Creative Print and Design (Wales),
Ebbw Vale.

1 2 3 4 5 6 7 8 9 10 / 09 08 07 06

Derek Prince Ministries—UK
Kingsfield, Hadrian Way, Baldock, SG7 6AN
United Kingdom

www.dpmuk.org

Contents

Derek Prince (1915-2003) was born in Bangalore, India, into a British military family. He was educated as a scholar of classical languages at Eton College and Cambridge University in England and later at Hebrew University, Israel. As a student, he was a philosopher and self-proclaimed atheist.

While in the British Medical Corps during World War II, Prince began to study the Bible as a philosophical work. Converted through a powerful encounter with Jesus Christ, he was baptized in the Holy Spirit a few days later. This life-changing experience altered the whole course of his life, which he thereafter devoted to studying and teaching the Bible as the Word of God.

Discharged from the army in Jerusalem in 1945, he married Lydia Christensen, founder of a children's home there. Upon their marriage, he immediately became father to Lydia's eight adopted daughters—six Jewish, one Palestinian Arab, one English. Together the family saw the rebirth of the state of Israel in 1948.

Lydia Prince died in 1975, and Derek married Ruth Baker, (a single mother to three adopted children) in 1978. He met his second wife, like his first, while he was serving the Lord in Jerusalem. Ruth died in December 1998 in Jerusalem where they had lived since 1981.

Derek Prince taught and ministered on six continents for over seven decades. In 2002 he said, "It is my desire—and I believe the Lord's desire—that this ministry continue the work, which God began through me over sixty years ago, until Jesus returns."

Derek Prince Ministries is now an international organisation which continues to impact lives by providing important Bible teaching to equip the worldwide church. His teaching has been translated into more than 60 languages and is equally relevant and helpful to people from all racial and religious backgrounds.

Marriage Is a Covenant

Do you have a successful marriage—one that brings you genuine happiness and satisfaction? Or—if you are not married yourself—how about your friends? How many couples do you know who have the kind of marriage that you would wish to have if you were married?

I remember a conversation with a young man who had come to me for help with his marriage. He was a minister in a large and well-known denomination. His experience in the ministry had left him sadly disillusioned. He said to me, "I know about forty couples well. Several of them are in the ministry with me. But to tell you the truth, I can't think of one couple that is really happy." Some people would call that cynical, but in some places it is realistic.

I want to share with you that it truly is possible to have a successful marriage. There is a key to such a marriage. I know, because I have found it. This book is based on experience, not merely on theory. It grieves me when I hear a so-called expert on marriage or the family holding forth in long, psychological jargon, yet when you examine their own lives, in many cases they too are the product of broken homes. Often they have at least one unsuccessful marriage in their past. A person needs to make it work in his own life before counselling, advising or helping others.

My first marriage with Lydia lasted almost thirty years. It was ended by her death in 1975. During our time together, we raised a family of nine daughters, so I know a little about raising children. We went through many hard experiences. We were in the middle of a war, the war that brought the state of Israel to birth. We faced a siege, famine and danger. We moved from country to country and continent to continent. We worked in Africa, Canada, Europe and in the United States. And our marriage was solid, happy and successful.

The success of a marriage does not depend on lack of tension or problems. It depends on establishing a relationship that can overcome those tensions and problems. The key to establishing such a relationship, simply put, is found in the Bible.

I believe that the Bible is a true, relevant, up-to-date book. It has the answers to life's problems. And I believe that when biblical truths are properly applied, they work. The Bible attaches great importance to marriage—much more, I believe, than many churchgoers realize.

According to the Bible, human history started with a marriage. God created Adam and then He said that it was not good for him to be alone. God formed and brought to him a wife. Thus, marriage initiated in the heart of God, not in the thoughts of man.

Fittingly, the Bible also ends with marriage. The great climax of all human history is the marriage supper of the Lamb. Now you can understand why I believe that—if you view it objectively—the Bible places tremendous importance on marriage.

In Ephesians 5 Paul spoke about marriage. He had been comparing the relationship of Jesus Christ and His Church to that of a bridegroom and his bride (verses 22-32). He concluded this comparison with this statement: "This is a great mystery." One of the other modern translations says, "a profound mystery" (NIV). He is speaking about marriage.

In the language of the New Testament, the word *mystery* had a specific meaning. It meant a secret that most people did not know but that could be learned if you went through a process of initiation. That is what marriage is. It is a secret that most people do not know, but it can be learned if you go through the process of initiation.

In the time of the prophet Malachi, Israel as a nation was not very close to God. God had given them His law but, in most cases, they had been somewhat disobedient and, as a result, they were not enjoying the blessings that God had promised them. Some of their problems were like the problems of many people today: dysfunctional families, marital stress, strained relationships. God puts His finger on the reason for their problems:

> *"This is another thing you do: you cover the altar of the LORD with tears, with weeping and with groaning, because He no longer regards the offering or accepts it with favour from your hand."*
> Malachi 2:13, NASB

These were religious people. They were doing plenty of praying, but God was not answering their prayers. So they asked, "For what reason?" Then the Lord gave them this answer:

> *"Because the LORD has been a witness between you and the wife of your youth, against whom you have dealt treacherously, though she is your companion and your wife by covenant."*
> verse 14, NASB

I want you to notice three points about these two verses. First of all, religion does not necessarily produce successful marriages. These people were very religious; they were praying all the time. They were in the temple, but their homes were in a mess. Sound familiar?

The second point is that a wrong relationship between a husband and wife hinders a relationship with God. God said He would not hear their prayers and they asked why. Then He said to them, "Because you haven't dealt right with your wife."

In the New Testament, Peter reaffirms the point. In 1 Peter 3, he instructs husbands to be careful how they live with their wives so that their prayers will not be hindered (verse 7). In other words, if you pray out of an unhappy marriage—out of a home that is out of order—your prayer may not be very effective. God says to get your home in order.

The third point is the vital one—it is the key. It is the last word of that Scripture, the word "covenant." This is the key to a successful marriage. It is the realization, understanding and acceptance—from Scripture—that marriage is a covenant. Covenant is one of the key concepts of the Bible. The same word that is translated "covenant" is also translated "testament". The entire Bible comes to us in the form of two covenants. What a demonstration of the importance God attaches to a covenant.

There are two essential features to a covenant that affect marriage:

1. A covenant demands commitment—total, unreserved, wholehearted commitment. Marriage is not an experimental relationship; it is not a trial. It can only succeed on the basis of total commitment.

2. In a covenant, God sets the terms for commitment. Man does not set the terms. This was the problem with Israel in the days of Malachi. They were trying to set their terms for how marriage should be and God said, "I won't accept that."

Laying Down Your Life

The Bible reveals that marriage is a covenant, and that a covenant demands commitment. There is no covenant without a commitment. Furthermore, in a covenant God sets the terms. He does not leave it to man to decide on what basis a marriage will be ordered.

In the Bible, a covenant always required a sacrifice—specifically the taking of a life. In the Old Testament, there was a rather strange method by which people entered into covenant with one another. They would take the sacrificial animals, slay them, cut them into halves, lay the two halves opposite one another and then walk together through the two halves of the slain animal. There is a very interesting example of this in Genesis 15, where the Lord Himself made a covenant with Abraham in this way.

You may think this is simply the case in the Old Testament, but that is not so. In Hebrews, the writer reinforces the requirement of sacrifice in the New Testament:

> *For where a covenant is, there must of necessity be the death of the one who made it. For a covenant is valid only when men are dead, for it is never in force while the one who made it lives.*
> Hebrews 9:16-17, NASB

What a startling statement! A covenant is only valid when the one who makes the covenant is dead. For us, as Christians, the great and final sacrifice is the death of Jesus. There are many passages of the New Testament that speak about this. For instance, in 2 Corinthians Paul says:

> *For the love of Christ controls us, having concluded this, that one died for all, therefore all died; and He died for all, so that they who live might no longer live for themselves, but for Him who died and rose again on their behalf.*
> 2 Corinthians 5:14-15, NASB

The sacrifice on which the New Covenant is based is the death of Jesus Christ on our behalf. And His death—when we accept it by faith—becomes our death. One died for all, therefore all were dead.

Christ did not die for Himself; He died for us. He died as our representative. His death becomes our death.

> *Now if we have died with Christ, we believe that we shall also live with Him, knowing that Christ, having been raised from the dead, is never to die again; death no longer is master over Him. For the death that He died, He died to sin once for all; but the life that He lives, He lives to God. Even so consider yourselves to be dead to sin, but alive to God in Christ Jesus.*
> Romans 6:8-11, NASB

The essential teaching about the death of Jesus Christ is that it was the last and final sacrifice for sin and that His death was substitutionary. He died for us, and so we enter into the New Covenant—not through two halves of a slain animal, but through the death of Jesus Christ on our behalf. But the covenant is only valid if we accept His death as our death. A covenant is not yet valid as long as the one who makes it lives. Jesus died to make the covenant with us but the covenant only becomes effective in our lives when we reckon ourselves to be dead with Him. His death becomes our death. He is the sacrifice through whom we pass into the New Covenant.

If marriage is a covenant between a man and a woman, a husband and a wife, how does this principle of covenant apply? The sacrifice upon which the covenant of Christian marriage is based is the death of Jesus Christ on our behalf. He is the sacrifice through which, by faith, a man and a woman can pass into the relationship of marriage as God Himself ordained that it should be. Just as the Lord and Abram passed between the pieces of the slain animals, so in Christian marriage a man and woman pass through the death of Jesus Christ on their behalf into a totally new life and a totally new relationship that would have been impossible without the death of Jesus Christ. The covenant of Christian marriage is made at the foot of the cross.

There are three successive phases in the outworking of this relationship. First, a life is laid down; each lays down his life for the other. The husband looks back at Christ's death on the cross, and says, "That death was my death. When I came through the cross, I died. Now I am no longer living for myself." The wife likewise looks at the cross and says the same: "That death was my death. When I came through the cross, I died. Now I am no longer living for myself."

Henceforth, each holds nothing back from the other. Everything the husband has is for the wife; everything the wife has is for the husband. No reservations. Nothing held back. It is a merger, not a partnership.

Second, out of that death comes a new life; each now lives out that new life in and through the other. The husband says to the wife, "My life is in you. I am living out my life through you. You are the expression of what I am." Likewise the wife says to the husband, "My life is in you. I am living out my life through you. You are the expression of what I am."

Third, the covenant is consummated by physical union. This in turn brings forth fruit that continues the new life that each has been willing to share with the other. In the realm of living creatures, God has ordained this basic principle: union brings forth fruit. Covenant leads to shared life and fruitfulness; life that is not shared remains sterile and fruitless.

This approach to marriage—which sees it in terms of a covenant—is very different from the attitude with which most people today enter into marriage. The attitude of our contemporary culture is more often, "What can I get? What's in it for me?" I believe that any relationship approached with this attitude is doomed to end in failure. The one who approaches marriage as a covenant does not ask, "What can I get?" but rather, "What can I give?" And the only valid answer must be: "I give my life. I lay it down for you, and then I find my new life in you." This applies equally to each party—to the husband and to the wife. To the natural mind this sounds ridiculous. Yet it is, in fact, the secret of real life, real happiness, and real love.

In marriage, there is a life to lose and a life to find. As long as you enter into marriage holding on to your own life, you will not find the life that God has for you in that covenant. It is a step of faith. You must lay down your life in faith and find a new life—a life that is different, a life that comes through union, a life that you cannot have on your own. Each party to the marriage has to make that step of faith.

The key word, again, is commitment. It is not an experiment. Commitment releases God's grace. Without God's grace, marriage will never work. But God does not release His grace into a marriage until both parties have made that commitment. And out of God's grace come the resources needed to make the marriage work.

Union That Leads to Knowing

The attitude of most people in our culture today is: "What can I get? What's in this for me?" I see this in nearly every circumstance, but especially with regard to marriage. I believe there must be a radical change of thinking for a man and a woman who together want to make their marriage succeed.

What is the unique end purpose of marriage? What is it that is made possible only through marriage and cannot be achieved in any other way? As you read this, if you are married, I want you to ask yourself, "Am I achieving that or am I missing the real purpose?"

Let's look at part of a conversation Jesus had with some of the Pharisees about marriage. It is recorded in Matthew 19:3-6:(NASB)

> *Some Pharisees came to Jesus, testing Him, and asking, "Is it lawful for a man to divorce his wife for any reason at all?" And He answered and said, "Have you not read that He who created them from the beginning made them male and female, and said, 'For this reason a man shall leave his father and mother and be joined to his wife, and the two shall become one flesh'? So they are no longer two, but one flesh. What therefore God has joined together, let no man separate."*

The teaching of some rabbis at the time was that a man could divorce his wife for any reason. They were doing what God does not accept: They were setting their own terms for the covenant of marriage.

Jesus' answer to the Pharisees, however, raises two important points. First, when Jesus taught about marriage, He went back to God's purpose at creation. He would not lower the standard to anything that had intervened in history from that time. He was faithful to His Father. He knew from the Scriptures, as all good Jews should know, the story of creation and of how God provided a mate for Adam. He said that is God's original purpose—the only purpose that is acceptable in God's sight.

When we talk about marriage as Christians, we need to do the same as Jesus: go back to the original purpose of God and see what that was.

Secondly, I want to point out what that purpose was: that two shall become one. Union. Unity is God-like. The ultimate, the original, the only perfect pattern of unity is found in the Godhead. The Father and the Son are one. Not one person, but one in union through the Holy Spirit. And, in a certain sense, what God is aiming at in marriage is that a man and a woman will achieve this most God-like of all achievements: true union, true unity. But the way to unity is the way that God has laid down. There is no other way but God's way into the kind of union God desires in marriage.

Union, in turn, leads to knowing. This is a thought that it is possibly difficult for people in our culture to understand because we have such an intellectual concept of what "knowing" is. In the original language of Scripture, the word *know* had a much deeper meaning than merely knowing facts.

In Genesis 4—immediately after the description of man's fall and its consequences—the chapter opens with this statement: "Adam knew Eve his wife" (verse 1, NKJV). The other modern translations tend to use some phrase like "Adam had relations with his wife." Of course, that is correct in the sense that it describes what happened, but the New King James

Version actually is more faithful to the original text. It points out that what God is aiming at is "knowing." Of course, between a husband and a wife that includes the sexual relationship. But merely to limit it to a sexual relationship is to miss the purpose of God. The New King James translation says: "Adam knew his wife." It was not merely sexual.

In the language of the Old Testament there were two distinct phrases used. One says a man "knew" a woman; the other says a man "lay" with a woman. And the Bible is very discriminating in how it uses those phrases. So God is being very specific when He tells us that the end purpose of marriage—through union—is that a man and a woman truly know one another.

The more I meditate on this, the more deep and wonderful it seems to me. In Mark 8:36-37, Jesus speaks about the worth of the human soul and He says, in fact, one human soul is worth more than the whole world. I believe that. I believe there is no way to measure the value of a single human soul. And marriage—as planned by God—opens the way for two human souls to know each other to their innermost depths in every area of their lives—physical, mental, emotional and cultural. Marriage is the union of two persons, not just two bodies, not just two minds. Some people put all the emphasis on sex; some put it all on the intellect. But in God's purpose it is total—a total knowing by one person of another. I speak from having been in two very happy marriages: one that lasted thirty years and another that lasted for nearly twenty years. In my personal judgment, there is no greater privilege in life than to be permitted to know another person in this way.

By insisting on a covenant and commitment as a way into marriage, God has provided protection for each party from being exploited or betrayed. Any people who allow themselves to have sexual relations without first making a covenant commitment are really prostituting their personalities. This goes deeper than terms of sexual morality. I believe in actual fact that person is desecrating the most precious thing that he or she has: their personality. They are exposing their entire personality to someone who is not willing to pay the price that God requires.

The purpose of marriage is a deep, ongoing, intimate, personal relationship protected by commitment. This relationship should be continually deeper and richer as the marriage continues.

I look back on my own first marriage and I think that for over thirty years Lydia and I were continually coming to know one another more deeply and more intimately. Our marriage grew richer and fuller the longer it lasted. Sometimes we would travel in the car together for an hour or more without speaking, and then—when we both began to speak simultaneously—we would start talking about exactly the same thing. In other words, the relationship did not just depend on verbal communion, nor did it depend merely upon sexual relationship. It was a total knowing of one person by another.

Counterfeits That Cheat Us

Human personality is the most precious and wonderful thing created in the universe. So God has set very careful boundaries so that one person may know another but not exploit the other. And those who ignore these boundaries and try to get the benefits without meeting the conditions are deceiving themselves. They are being cheated. Let's examine these counterfeits that cheat us—human substitutes for marriage that do not produce God's result. People only counterfeit things that are valuable, and this applies to marriage. If it were not so valuable, there would be no counterfeits.

When the Old Testament speaks about a man having sexual relationship with a woman it uses two distinct phrases. In some places it says the man "knew" the woman; in other places it says the man "lay" with the woman. If you care to trace this, you will see that there is a careful distinction maintained. The Bible usually says that a man "knew" a woman if the relationship was legitimate—if it was in line with God's ordinance for sexual relationship between a man and a woman, if it was based on a covenant commitment. But if a man merely had sexual relationship with a woman without making a covenant commitment to her, it does not say that the man "knew" the woman, but usually says he "lay" with her.

This contains the deep truth that God does not open the way for the kind of interpersonal relationship where one person truly "knows" another unless it is preceded by covenant commitment. There can be physical relationship, there can be some kind of sexual pleasure, but the real purpose of marriage—the deep, inner knowing of two persons, one of the other—is possible only on the basis of covenant commitment.

> *Marriage is to be held in honour among all, and the marriage bed is to be undefiled; for fornicators and adulterers God will judge.*
> Hebrews 13:4, NASB

This is a statement that cannot be challenged. God is going to judge fornicators and adulterers. Fornication is having sexual relationship without a covenant commitment—promiscuous sex. Adultery is what happens when a person makes a covenant commitment in marriage and then breaks the commitment by having a relationship with someone outside the marriage. Of the two sins, adultery is a greater sin than fornication because it is the breaking of that most sacred agreement: a covenant. But in each case, the sin consists of a wrong attitude toward covenant commitment. One is trying to get the relationship without the covenant commitment; the other is making a covenant commitment and then breaking it.

God's requirements are designed to protect us from being hurt. When you indulge in illegitimate sex, you are desecrating your own personality. And the ultimate end of that is not satisfaction nor joy nor peace. It is frustration and hurt.

> *Flee immorality. Every other sin that a man commits is outside the body, but the immoral man sins against his own body.*
> 1 Corinthians 6:18, NASB

I do not believe that this merely means that a person who indulges in promiscuous sex is liable to contract a sexually transmitted disease. I believe that a person who indulges in illegitimate sex is misusing and abusing his or her own body. And our bodies protest against that misuse. The results that come from abusing the sexual relationship become evident in our total personality.

We sometimes speak about people breaking God's laws. I do not believe that is accurate. We never break God's laws; God's laws break us. It is true in the physical realm. No one has ever yet broken the law of gravity. A person can step out of a fourth floor window. But what happens? They do not break the law of gravity; the law of gravity breaks them. I believe that is exactly how it is in this matter of sexual relationships. We do not break God's laws; God's laws break us.

The essence of lust is using a human personality as a means of momentary physical satisfaction—not appreciating the personality in itself, but simply exploiting it for another purpose. God never deals with human personality in this way. God always respects the personality that He Himself created.

Let's look at two vivid descriptions of what lust is and what it does. The first is taken from Proverbs 7:6-27 of The Living Bible:

> *I was looking out the window of my house one day and saw a simple-minded lad, a young man lacking common sense, walking at twilight down the street to the house of this wayward girl, a prostitute. She approached him, saucy and pert, and dressed seductively. She was the brash, coarse type, seen often in the streets and markets, soliciting at every corner for men to be her lovers.*
>
> *She put her arms around him and kissed him, and with a saucy look she said, "I was just coming to look for you and here you are! . . . my bed is spread with lovely, coloured sheets of finest linen imported from Egypt, perfumed with myrrh, aloes and cinnamon. Come on, let's take our fill of love until*

morning, for my husband is away on a long trip. He has taken a wallet full of money with him and won't return for several days."

So she seduced him with her pretty speech, her coaxing and her wheedling, until he yielded to her. He couldn't resist her flattery. He followed her as an ox going to the butcher or as a stag that is trapped, waiting to be killed with an arrow through its heart. He was as a bird flying into a snare, not knowing the fate awaiting it there.

Listen to me, young men, and not only listen but obey; don't let your desires get out of hand; don't let yourself think about her. Don't go near her; stay away from where she walks, lest she tempt you and seduce you. For she has been the ruin of multitudes—a vast host of men have been her victims. If you want to find the road to hell, look for her house.

Proverbs 7:6-27, TLB

That is plain speaking, but it is the truth. If you are inclined to say, "Well, that's religious. That's the way religious people think," I want you to read the words of another man, one of the greatest masters of the English language: William Shakespeare. Shakespeare was not (as far as we know) a religious man, but he was a master of descriptive language and a very accurate observer of human life. This is what Shakespeare had to say in one of his sonnets on lust:

> The expense of spirit and the waste of shame
> Is lust in action, and till action, lust
> Is perjur'd, murderous, bloody, full of blame,
> Savage, extreme, rude, cruel, not to trust,
> Enjoy's no sooner but despised straight,
> Past reason hated, as a swallowed bait,
> On purpose laid to make the taker mad:
> Mad in pursuit, and in possession so,

Had, having, and in quest to have, extreme,
A bliss in proof, and prov'd, a very woe,
Before, a joy propos'd, behind, a dream;
All this the world well knows, yet none knows well
To shun the heaven that leads men to this hell.

I do not think anybody has ever described lust more vividly or accurately than this—especially those last two lines. What kind of heaven is it that leads men to hell? It is a false heaven, a counterfeit. It is the devil's, and it leads you to destruction.

How can you escape that hell? Shakespeare says, "No one knows well to shun the heaven that leads men to this hell." Here is how you can shun that false heaven of deceptive lust: Order your life according to God's law. Accept what God says about the sanctity of the body and the sanctity of marriage. Let marriage be honourable in all, the bed undefiled. Do not sin against your own body by immorality. God is right. He tells us the truth. He set these fences and boundaries to our conduct for our own good. We only rebel against them to our own destruction.

The Roles of Husband and Wife

According to God's pattern, marriage is a covenant in which each party lays down his life for the other and then lives out a new life through the other. Still, we must resist human substitutes that do not produce God's result. As we do that day by day, we also rely on the Holy Spirit to empower us to walk out our God-appointed roles as husband and wife—the special contribution that each party makes to the total relationship.

As I see it in Scripture, the husband has three basic responsibilities toward his wife: first, to be a head; second, to provide; and third, to protect. In 1 Corinthians 11:3, Paul says, "The man is the head of a woman" (NAS). What does it mean to be the "head"? I believe it implies ultimate responsibility for decision and direction. Obviously the term "head" is taken from the physical body and in the physical body—as I understand the way God has ordered it—decision and direction come from the head. Through the central nervous system, all parts of the body can communicate with the head, but the head is responsible for making decisions and issuing direction. I believe that is the ultimate responsibility of the husband: to lead.

> But if any one does not provide for his own, and especially for those of his household, he has denied the faith and is worse than an unbeliever.
> 1 Timothy 5:8, NASB

That is very strong language to say that somebody is worse than an unbeliever and has denied the Christian faith. What kind of person is Paul speaking about? He is speaking about a man who does not provide for his wife and family.

It is a sad fact, but there are quite a large number of people who call themselves Christians and put on "a spiritual act," but have not made proper provision for their own families. The Bible says that is worse than being an unbeliever.

Provision, of course, is primarily financial. We use the phrase "the breadwinner." However, I do not believe that a husband's provision for his wife is limited to finance. I believe that he is responsible for her total well being: physical, emotional, social and cultural. I believe it is his responsibility to see that all her legitimate needs are met. Paul said the wife is the husband's glory. In other words, if you want to know how successful a man is, look at his wife. She is the evidence. And when a wife is fully provided for in every area of her life—physical emotional, social and cultural—she will indeed be her husband's glory.

The third responsibility of the man is to protect.

> You husbands in the same way, live with your wives in an understanding way, as with someone weaker, since she is a woman; and grant her honour as a fellow heir of the grace of life, so that your prayers will not be hindered.
> 1 Peter 3:7, NASB

Now that is one of the passages where the Bible goes contrary to most people's thinking, because the attitude of natural man is, if someone is weak, you dominate. You can get your way, you can force your way through. But the Scripture says, just because the woman is weak, that is the reason not to dominate but to honour.

Peter says that the husband and wife are heirs together of

the grace of life—joint-heirs. This is very significant because in the legal system during Bible days, when two people were joint-heirs, neither of them could claim the inheritance apart from the other. Claiming their inheritance depended upon them operating together and moving together into their inheritance.

This is true of husband and wife. There are many parts of God's provision which a wife or husband cannot claim on their own. It is only as they learn to flow together and to harmonize that the full provision of God is made available. So it is a husband's business to protect his wife, to stand between her and every pressure, every blow, everything that would break her down. And husband, the more you protect your wife, the more joy and satisfaction you receive in return from her. It pays to invest in your wife.

Regarding the wife, in Genesis 2 where God introduces the theme of marriage, He describes what He intends the wife to be: a helper. I believe that sums up in one word the real purpose of God for the wife. It is to be her husband's helper. I suggest there are two primary ways in which a wife can help her husband. The first is to uphold; the second is to encourage.

How can a wife uphold her husband? The easiest way to understand that is to again picture the physical body. We have established that the head is the directive, decision-making part of the body. And yet the head never holds itself up. The head is totally dependent upon the rest of the body to be upheld and sustained and nourished. And there is one particular part of the body that is closest to the head and has the direct responsibility for upholding the head: the neck. In a certain sense, a wife could picture herself as the neck—the part that is immediately responsible for upholding the head. If you find that a little unsettling or undignified, bear in mind what somebody once said that it is the neck that determines just which way the head will turn. There is a lot of truth in that!

Another way the wife can be a helper is to encourage. I cannot tell you how important it is for a man to be able to look to his wife for encouragement. I can remember times in my past when I felt I was a failure. And plenty of other people felt I was a failure, too. But I thank God that my first wife, Lydia, never, in any way, suggested to me that I was a failure. When I was down, she lifted me up. She encouraged me. I can remember one time I came to a point early in my ministry when I felt I never wanted to preach again. I went to bed totally discouraged. I woke up next morning feeling fine, ready to go. My wife had spent the whole night in prayer for me. I cannot thank God enough for a wife like that.

Wives, if you are going to encourage your husbands, you may need to practice a fair amount of self-denial. Suppose you are sitting there feeling dissatisfied—discontented with yourself, your husband, your home, your children, your car—but you know your husband is discouraged, too. What are you going to do? Are you going to tell him just how bad you feel and just how blue you are and just how much you need encouragement and help? That is where you have to deny yourself. At times you have to suppress your own discouragement, your own negative emotions, and devote yourself to encouraging your husband—telling him what a fine husband he is, how much you love him, how much good he is doing you. Think about everything you can that is good and focus on it. You might say, "Well, that's asking a lot." Maybe, but you will get a lot out of it too. In the end, you will always reap what you sow into your husband.

I would be less than honest if I did not warn you of the two common basic failures of husband and wife. When a marriage fails it is usually because either or both have failed in these ways.

The common failure of the husband in our culture today is the abdication of his responsibility—not to be the head, not to lead. Sometimes this is done in a very quiet way that is not seen. Nevertheless, it is a failure.

The wife's common failure is correspondent: to usurp responsibility—to take over headship. There is a great danger of a vicious circle in which the husband continually abdicates and the wife continually takes over more and more responsibility. The only way that they can receive the needed grace is through the covenant commitment that God establishes as the basis of marriage.

May God give you the grace to understand and implement these vital truths. It can mean the difference between success and failure in the most important human relationship of your life.

Books Available from Derek Prince Ministries

A complete list of Derek Prince's books, audio teachings and video teachings is available at www.dpmuk.org

Derek Prince Ministries
Worldwide Offices

AUSTRALIA
DPM—Australia
1st Floor, 134 Pendle Way
Pendle Hill
New South Wales 2145
Australia
Tel: + 612 9688 4488
Fax: + 612 9688 4848
Email: enquiries@au.derekprince.com

CANADA
DPM—Canada
P.O. Box 8354
Halifax, Nova Scotia B3K 5M1
Canada
Tel: + 1 902 443 9577
Fax: + 1 902 443 6013
E-mail: dpmcanada@compuserve.com

FRANCE
DPM—France
Route d'Oupia, B.P. 31
34210 Olonzac
France
Tel: + 33 468 913872
Fax: + 33 468 913863
Email: 106317.3002@compuserve.com

GERMANY
DPM—Germany
Schwarzauer Str. 56
D-83308 Trostberg
Tel: + 49 8621 64146
Fax: + 49 8621 64147
E-mail: IBL.de@t-online.de

NETHERLANDS
DPM—Netherlands
P.O. Box 349
1960 AH Heemskerk
The Netherlands
Tel: + 31 251 255 044
Fax: + 31 251 247 798
E-mail: enquiries@nl.derekprince.com

SINGAPORE
Derek Prince Publications Pte. Ltd.
P.O. Box 2046
Robinson Road Post Office
Singapore 904046
Tel: + 65 6392 1812
Fax: + 65 6392 1823
Email: dpmchina@singnet.com.sg

SOUTH AFRICA
DPM—South Africa
P.O. Box 33367
Glenstantia 0010 Pretoria
South Africa
Tel: +27 12 348 9537
Fax: + 27 12 348 9538
E-mail: dpmsa@mweb.co.za

SOUTH PACIFIC
DPM—South Pacific
PO Box 2029
Christchurch 8015
New Zealand
Tel: + 64 3 366 4443
Fax: + 64 3 366 1569
E-mail: secretary@dpm.co.nz

Derek Prince Ministries
Worldwide Offices

SWITZERLAND
DPM—Switzerland
Alpenblick 8
8934 Knonau
Switzerland
Tel: + 41(0) 44 768 25 06
E-mail: dpm-ch@ibl-dpm.net

UNITED KINGDOM
DPM—UK
Kingsfield
Hadrian Way
Baldock
Hertfordshire SG7 6AN
UK
Tel: + 44 (0) 1462 492100
Fax: + 44 (0) 1462 492102
Email: enquiries@dpmuk.org

USA
DPM—USA
PO Box 19501
Charlotte
NC 28219-9501
USA
Tel: + 1 704 357 3556
Fax: + 1 704 357 1413
E-mail: ContactUs@derekprince.org

If you have enjoyed reading this book and are interested in going deeper into the Word of God, then join our informal network of individuals, pastors and lay leaders interested in learning how to grow in their faith and respond to challenges of daily life.

To join and receive the following teaching message FREE OF CHARGE, fill out this form and send in an envelope to our address below.

Total Security

A Christian's security is through right relationships: (a) with God, (b) with our fellow-man. This is provided by God's eternal plan for us.

Preferred format: ☐ CD ☐ Tape ☐ MP3* (Code: 4237)

* Please supply email address

Name _____

Address _____

_____Postcode _____

Tel _____

E-mail* _____

Role in the local church: ☐ Member ☐ Lay Leader ☐ Pastor ☐ None

Age: ☐ 18–25 ☐ 26–35 ☐ 36–45 ☐ 46–55 ☐ 56–65 ☐ 65+

Marital Status: ☐ Single ☐ Married ☐ Widowed ☐ Divorced

When it comes to learning, which medium is your favourite:

☐ Books ☐ Tapes ☐ CDs ☐ MP3 ☐ Video ☐ DVD

Number of Christian books you purchased in last year: ☐ 1–5 ☐ 5–10 ☐ 10+

Do you listen/watch: ☐ UCB ☐ Premier ☐ God TV ☐ other _____

What Christian magazines do you read regularly? _____

What was the last great Christian book you read? _____

Derek Prince Ministries–UK
Kingsfield • Hadrian Way
Baldock • SG7 6AN • UK

Tel: +44 (0)1462 492100
Web: www.dpmuk.org
Email: enquiries@dpmuk.org
Reg Charity No. 327763

This is an introductory offer for those not already on our mailing list   T01RC